MINDFUL INTENTIONS

MINDFUL INTENTIONS

LOUIE SCHWARTZBERG and

M*I*RAVAL.

HAY HOUSE, INC.
Carlsbad, California • New York City
London • Sydney • Johannesburg
Vancouver • Hong Kong • New Delhi

Published and distributed in the United States by: Hay House, Inc.: www.hayhouse.com® • Published and distributed in Australia by:
Hay House Australia Pty. Ltd.: www.hayhouse.com.au • Published and distributed in the United Kingdom by: Hay House UK, Ltd.:
www.hayhouse.co.uk • Published and distributed in the Republic of South Africa by: Hay House SA (Pty), Ltd.: www.hayhouse.co.za •
Distributed in Canada by: Raincoast Books: www.raincoast.com • Published in India by: Hay House Publishers India: www.hayhouse.co.in

Produced by Stonesong
Cover and interior design: Vertigo Design NYC
Photographs: Louie Schwartzberg

Library of Congress Control Number: 2014930870

Hardcover ISBN: 978-1-4019-4611-1

10 9 8 7 6 5 4 3 2 1

1st edition, October 2014
Printed in China

For those who seek a moment to breathe.

CONTENTS

A NOTE FROM THE MIRAVAL OWNERS

Since our first arrival to Miraval a decade ago, and continuing since that day, we have been delighted to get to know the many practitioners, providers, and employees who bring the unique Miraval experience to life. All these individuals are passionate about how they contribute to the guest experience.

On the pages of this lovely book, you will find Louie Schwartzberg's astonishing images of Mother Nature's beauty married perfectly to the words shared by the amazing team at Miraval. It is our hope you will return to these pages whenever you need a moment to pause and be aware.

We believe what you hold in your hands is a mindfulness tool expressed in an exquisite, charming, and awe-inspiring way. We hope you will agree. Enjoy!

Steve and Jean Case

A WORD FROM MICHAEL TOMPKINS
CHIEF EXECUTIVE OFFICER, MIRAVAL RESORT & SPA

At Miraval Resort & Spa, we believe that setting an intention is the first step in making a choice to initiate an action.

While reading Facebook one day, I came across the highly acclaimed *Gratitude* video created by award-winning filmmaker Louie Schwartzberg, and I set an intention to connect with Louie and introduce him to Miraval. I felt that our philosophies aligned— particularly around nature and the appreciation of all human beings and wildlife—as they embodied mindfulness.

Most of us are blessed with five senses. If a sense is lost, the remaining ones become heightened to allow us the ability to be proficient in our environment. Oftentimes, because of overstimulation in today's frenetic, fast-paced world, our senses shut down to protect us from the chaos. At Miraval, we encourage our guests to live mindfully, enabling the senses to reopen and the beauty of taste, touch, smell, sound, and sight to reenergize our lives and bring us back into the present moment.

My intuition to connect with Louie led me to look up his company, BlackLight Films, on a Sunday afternoon. I wanted to leave a message for him, letting him know how moved I was by his powerful visuals and video short. As luck would have it, he answered the telephone.

We've now been blessed with having Louie's work assimilate into Miraval programming, both in photography and video. Our idea for *Mindful Intentions* came from the synergy of Miraval's mission and BlackLight's incredible visual imagery.

Our hope is that you will use this book and the accompanying video to help you take a meditative moment each day; set a Mindful Intention to protect yourself from the stress and chaos of everyday living; and open your world to brilliant, new possibilities.

A WORD FROM LOUIE SCHWARTZBERG

When I journey out to capture imagery, I intend to have my mind be as blank and sensitive as film itself, open to any subject without preconceived notions, always in a state of readiness, sitting in the dark waiting for light to strike.

When light energy enters my eyes, I seek a connection to the senses, to find a pathway that reaches the deepest part of my soul. That recognition of universal rhythms warms my heart because it is a homecoming event. It's a connection to a living universe that is comforting and loving. Every cell in my body rejoices at the reflection of seeing itself mirrored in the beauty of universal energy and the feeling of being at one with every living being from a micro-organism to a smiling face. It fills me with gratitude that I am alive, present, and mindful of this moment.

When Michael invited me to Miraval, I discovered there was an environment that nurtured the experience to awaken the senses. Since many of us are so busy trying to achieve our own missions or goals with the joy of serving others by sharing our passion for celebrating life, we at times ignore taking care of ourselves—our body, mind, and spirit. At Miraval, I encountered a dedicated team and an oasis that allowed the rejuvenation of the senses, the body to be energized, and—the greatest gift—peace of mind.

I'm overjoyed to add visual healing as another pathway to the heart. Nature makes us present, mindful, and connected. Nature's beauty is the conductor that orchestrates the symphony of life. We protect what we fall in love with. We realize that although we play only a small part in this grand performance, being a part of it engenders gratitude.

I hope these images will take you on your own personal journey of self-discovery, like a true explorer, but know that you don't have to travel around the world to experience this . . . just connect with the truth and beauty that is deep and precious inside yourself.

WHAT IS MINDFULNESS?

To be mindful is to live in the present moment. It sounds simple because it is simple, but human beings are complicated. We're wired to make things more complex than they are. So, the practice of mindfulness can take a good deal of effort . . . at first.

Like with all things, practice makes perfect, and being mindful is no different. Once it becomes a way of life, the results can be truly transformative. Health, well-being, compassion, happiness, and enlightenment can all be realized through mindfulness.

Miraval's mission is to inspire and encourage self-discovery and life balance through the practice of being mindful. Indeed, mindfulness is at the center of everything we do. Every one of our world-renowned specialists has his or her own unique approach to a mindful practice: meditation, outdoor challenges, integrative wellness, spiritual rituals, and intuition, to name a few. Many of these approaches will be celebrated in this book.

Buddha's word for mindfulness was *Vipassana*, meaning "the path to enlightenment." Vipassana has few rules except that, like any meaningful endeavor, it should begin with a deep breath. It has been said that by breathing deeply, we live deeply. Unfortunately, what is normal for most of us is shallow breathing, which keeps us from being truly open.

After that first deep breath is exhaled, mindfulness can take many forms. It can happen during a meditation session, or it can happen in the shower before you go to work. It has been described as a "mental flashlight," a conscious decision on where to put your focus. It isn't the past or the future; it is now. It is a choice. It is about observing and accepting everything that comes into your mind. The mind isn't always easy to calm, and that's all right. Strong emotions or anxious thoughts may come up, but you can still simply acknowledge them, rather than react to them.

Mindfulness isn't always born from calm and quiet. Indeed, sometimes, as with some of the outdoor challenges we offer our guests at Miraval, it is fear that catapults us into a heightened, in-the-moment state. Everything naturally slows down, and we're able to choose our response carefully through the sudden clarity of our instinctive inner voice. What follows is empowerment and confidence. This is an excellent example of mindfulness.

Meditation is the most widely recognized form of mindful practice. Research has shown that it can aid in reducing pain experienced by hospital patients, particularly for children, women in labor, and those undergoing cancer treatment. One especially powerful technique features the use of Healing Visualization. What is visualized is entirely up to the individual, as long as it helps one enter a meditative state. A common visualization choice is that of natural surroundings—a beach, forest, or meadow. There's something about the power of nature that sets the perfect stage for inner peace and joy. It reminds us that we're a part of something bigger, and fills us with gratitude—another key pathway to mindfulness.

The profound connection to nature as a way of being in the present moment is also the idea behind this book. Through the breathtaking photography of Louie Schwartzberg, you can take a moment to be mindful at any time of the day. Each photograph is paired with a Mindful Intention that can act as a meditative cue to help you shut out daily stresses and focus inward.

The meaning of *Miraval* is "view of the valley." At times, it's the view of the beauty all around us that helps us to better see the beauty that lies within.

WHAT IS A MINDFUL INTENTION?

Words are powerful. So much of who we are, what we do, and how we live is framed and forged by language. Even when the goal is to clear and calm the mind, words can be put to use very effectively. That is how we come to our Mindful Intentions.

A Mindful Intention is a word, phrase, or sentence that's used as a cue to help the mind focus, to shine that "mental flashlight" on a singular, purposeful thought. For example, mantras—which originated in Hindu philosophy and are associated with the practice of meditation—are Mindful Intentions. The most well-known and commonly used mantra is "Om," which is the source of all Hindu mantras. It symbolizes God—or a reflection of absolute reality, a reality that has no beginning and no end. It's believed that by chanting "ommm" at the beginning of a meditation, the sound of the word itself creates a vibration that evokes a divine energy and allows one to enter a higher state of consciousness.

Another example of a Mindful Intention is an invocation. Invocations are used in a variety of religious disciplines to call forth God, or a spiritual force. In Christianity, it is basically used to pray. Indeed, the Lord's Prayer is considered an invocation.

In this same spirit, at Miraval we use Mindful Intentions to turn inward and become centered. As it's reflected in the name, we use the words to help us become mindful, and we do so with a focused intent. The range of those intents can be vast. You may

need to heal your mind, body, and/or spirit, for instance. You may want to feel more gratitude. Maybe you simply want to let go of your body and mind completely, or release a specific anxiety or worry. Or perhaps you just want to feel joy. These Mindful Intentions, provided by Miraval specialists for this book, can be used as tools to help you live in the present moment. We created a wide variety so that you can focus on the now in a way that feels authentic to who you are.

Each of these Mindful Intentions has been paired with an inspiring photograph taken by Louie, who has spent a lifetime approaching film and photography from a state of mindfulness. In fact, he personally selected each photo with a corresponding Mindful Intention, taking both to a higher, more meaningful place. As powerful as words are, they can be even more empowering when used with visualization, and the visuals provided in the upcoming pages are truly transcendent.

It is our great hope that these Mindful Intentions will open doors for you, and encourage not only a mindful moment or two, but also a life in balance.

PEOPLE, PLACES, AND EXPERIENCES

The idea of being mindful threads through both Eastern and Western thought, and Miraval represents a crossroads where those different approaches meet and thrive.

Whether it's a nutritionist, an athletic coach who is also a psychotherapist, a professional outdoor and wilderness guide, a medical doctor trained as a shamanic/spiritual healer, or a horseman whose background is working with troubled adolescents, Miraval's team of specialists all have their own unique methods. Their combined wisdom helps to make the images on each page come to life in a variety of insightful ways.

And then, there is Louie Schwartzberg.

One look through Louie's eyes will immediately convince you that the compulsion to share his perspective on the world is not only inspired, but also desperately needed. As a child of two Holocaust survivors, Louie grew up with a heightened appreciation of the world around him. He began shooting nature films as a young man and quickly established himself as a world-renowned expert in time-lapse photography. Today, he is the only cinematographer in the world to have been shooting time-lapse photography continuously for over three decades, but he didn't stop there. Louie has also become a master at any and all ways of celebrating the natural world on film, including slice-of-life, aerial, 2-D, and 3-D photography. His award-winning work has been featured in films by acclaimed directors from Steven Spielberg to Francis Ford Coppola, and can be found in every imaginable platform from video shorts and documentaries, to full-length features and mobile apps.

The locations of the images you will encounter in this book cover the entire globe, but they all have one thing in common: Louie's own mindful intention. His intent is to approach each location and subject with an open mind, an open heart, and a sense of wonder. What he receives in return is astounding. It's the pure energy and power of the Iguazú Falls, which span the border between Argentina and Brazil, that teaches the lesson that life is unstoppable. It's the life-affirming harmony presented by the sensual swaying of 20,000 poppies in a field on the coast of Big Sur, California—all screaming to be loved in the tiny window of time that they have to flourish and pollinate. And, it's the crucial yet threatened symbiosis of the flower needing the bee to spread its DNA around Louie's backyard and beyond, creating the benefits of geographical diversity. However profound the message, it is always more than he hoped for, and through his exquisite work, we, too, are the fortunate recipients of these discoveries.

Louie's belief is that observing nature with humility and patience is like peeling an onion. Layer by layer, an entire universe of wisdom and possibility is gently revealed. Our intent is for you to experience this book in a similar way, allowing each page to uncover another magnificent path to mindfulness.

MINDFUL INTENTIONS

If you must know how something will come out before you begin, you will never start.

The sound of waves crashing is Mother Nature exhaling.

Every challenge that crashes in . . . in time, recedes.

I am mindfully aware of my thoughts as they flow through me. I celebrate choice.

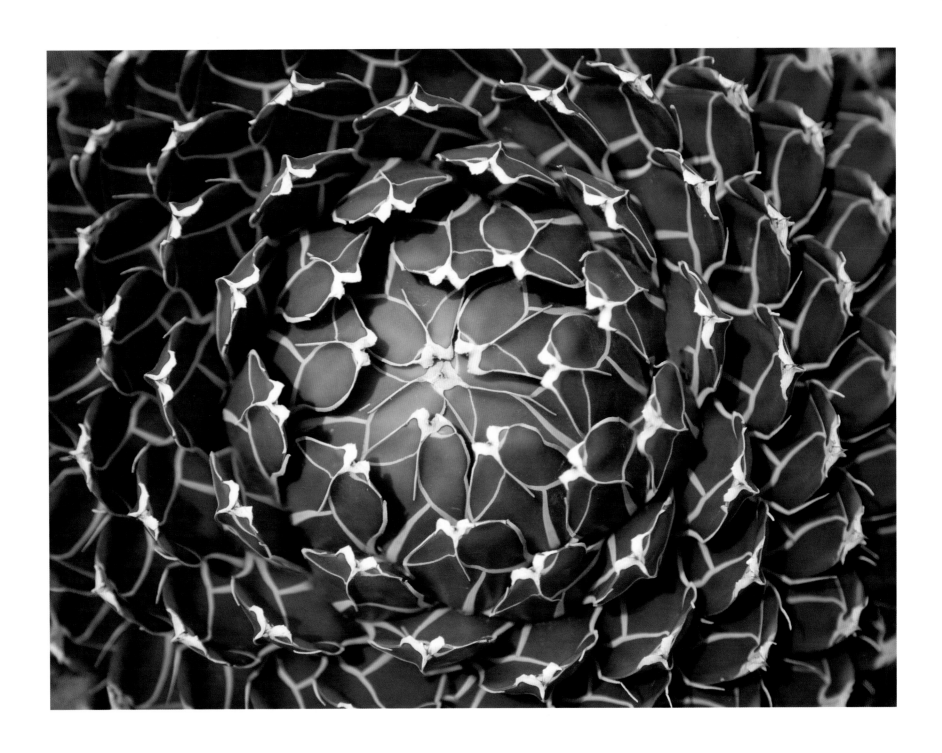

Nature's symmetry reflects balance and harmony.

Looking into the eyes of an animal reminds us that we share the journey as travelers on Earth.

I am not afraid of storms, for I am learning how to sail my ship.

The way to make any sense out of change is to join the dance.

Nature never takes more than what it needs. It is all about efficiency and symbiotic relationships.

Balance is not something to be found or achieved; it is something
you do by constantly returning to your center.

Patterns and systems in civilization mirror the ecosystems in nature.

We have the choice and the power to make every day amazing.

Joy has the power of light. When we bask in it, we see ever so clearly.

Experience the grandeur that only nature can provide.

Remember that getting out of your comfort zone, by definition, is going to be uncomfortable.

Permanent change is slow change made real with small steps.

Be aware of the foods you desire and those that you require.

Discover truth and beauty through nature's universal patterns and rhythms.

The challenge is the journey. The journey can yield the greatest rewards.

There are no limitations in life—they exist only in our minds.

Laughter is energy for the soul.

If you worry about where you're going, you might miss the beauty of where you are.

Rediscover nature through the eyes of a child.

Be curious. Life has so much to teach.

We only have to walk out into nature to be reminded that we are not alone.

Life is all about symbiotic relationships.

To find wisdom, listen.

Embrace the beauty of nature, and there you will find peace.

Watching a flower's gentle unfolding can open the wonders of the world.

Nature's beauty opens your heart to profound wonder and compassion.

No music exists that is more pleasing than the sounds of nature.

When deep in the cold of winter, I am grateful,
for I know that spring will soon follow.

I am 100 percent responsible for 50 percent of every relationship I am in.

A rose needs tending beyond the bloom.
Don't abandon what you cultivate.

There is beauty in every season of life.

Anchoring in the present moment, I feel my breath and my feet at the same time.

Life is bountiful. Greet it with gratitude.

Reconnect to life with hope and meaning.

Dream to find the way by moonlight, and see the dawn before the rest of the world.

An inquisitive mind can unveil the mysteries of the world.

Don't waste energy on things that are out of your control.
If you stay focused, you can do anything.

The formation of clouds will never be the same as before . . . just like this moment.

You have to live to learn.

The sound of a bird's song is a gentle reminder that life exists beyond your window.

Life is as fragile as the wings of a butterfly.

Life is a powerful, unstoppable force of energy.

We are connected to a living universe.

There is strength in unity.

If you want to grow, expand, and know who you are,
you must explore uncharted territories.

Change happens when the discomfort of the familiar outweighs the fear of the unknown.

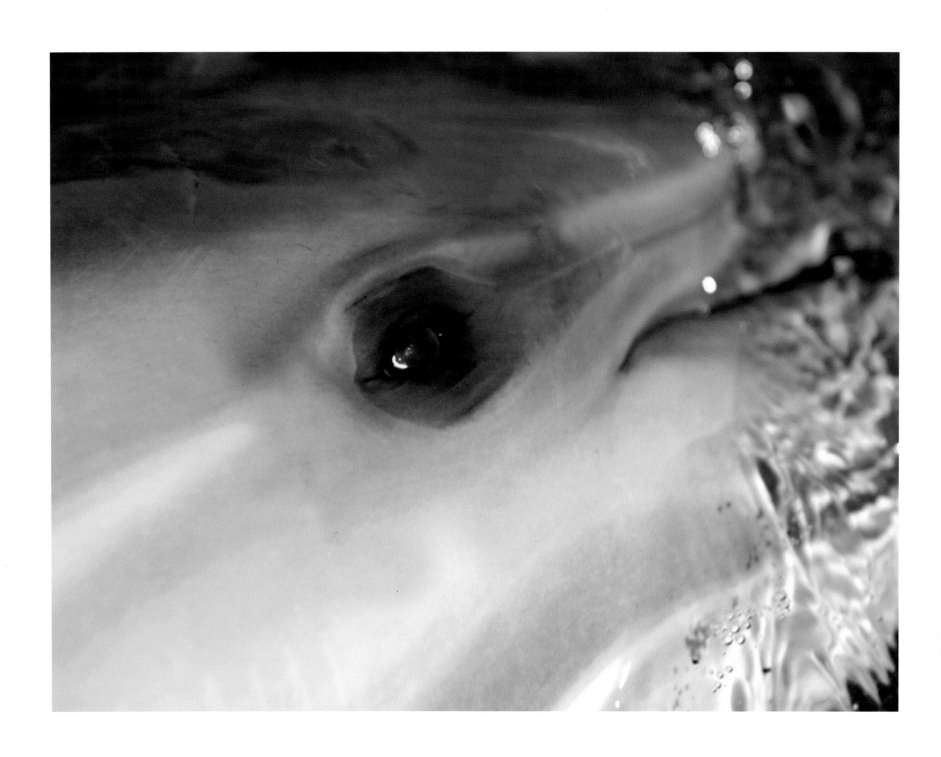

To sustain life on the planet, have respect for all living creatures.

Trust emergence.

I am a movement unto myself.
Energy is not something I burn; it is a force that I create.

Trust is the very first step.

The more time passes, the more each moment,
each day, shines with golden light.

Love more.

Today, I will not worry about the future or regret the past.
I will face the shadows and be the light. Today is my day. I own it.

If what you are doing has not produced any definitive changes, it is not working.
Know when it is time to break free from your own practices.

Even the most foreboding barriers tumble away when
faced with the power of truth and love.

Life reflects how we are interconnected to a changing universe.

Nature makes me feel humble, reverent, and inspired.

Be curious, and explore new horizons through nature.

Nature fills me with wonder and wisdom while opening my heart.

My heart jumps for joy watching flowers come alive, dancing to the light.

A love connection is everlasting.

Forget your past. Let go of your future.
Open your present—it is a gift.

Gratitude creates a shift in perception.

Mindfulness 101: Slow down, tune in, and breathe.

Celebrate all the gifts that nature provides.

For change to occur, you must start where you are.
Recognize the value of each incremental step instead of just focusing on the outcome you want.

Nature opens the heart.

I will not let today pass by quietly or unappreciated.
I will treat today as if it were my very first and live it as if it were my very last.

The heart pumps blood to itself, first.

Look within to find happiness.

Today, if an opportunity is not in front of me, I will let go of any doubts and find one. I will challenge my fears.

View your world through a different lens.

Of the blessings set before you, make your choice and be content.

Speed does not equate urgency. Just because our devices allow instant communication, it does not mean that urgent action is required. False urgency creates stress.

Today, my focus is squarely on the three things I can control:
me, myself, and I.

Begin each day by asking: What is my purpose in life?
How can I fulfill that purpose today?

The quickest path to stress and feeling overwhelmed is trying to do too much while holding on to unreasonable expectations.

If you feel invisible, wear brighter colors,
and touch another life in a positive way, every day.

Do not dwell in the past; do not dream of the future. Concentrate on the present moment.

Choose happiness.

The existence of a flower is nature's way of saying,
"Look at me! Look at me!"

Nature does not waste a single molecule.

Exercise regularly.

Enjoy the ecstatic moments in life.

Grief is a healthy, natural response to all kinds of losses.
Grief is a process that time heals.

Let life live through you.

Imagine the life you want to live—then live it.

No amount of money will buy a 25-year-old
what 50 years of living has given me.

*Today, I will strive to make a positive difference in my family,
my community, and my world.*

It is only a view if you come home to it.

Get out of your mind by getting into your body.

Sunny or cloudy—it does not matter.
Today I will encourage my heart to sing.

A flower blooming is an invitation to love.

Each day I am grateful to my sight—that I can see the beauty of a flower.

Breathing, eating, and loving are essential components of life,
which is reason enough to be more deliberate about all three.

When you get to the other side, there is only one thing waiting . . . joy!

Love is a wondrous thing, and it is always best when shared.

If I ask for what I want and accept what I receive,
I will get what I need.

Why can't we sit down and talk about what we are afraid of?
Because we are afraid of the truth. Today I will face my fears and open myself to the truth.

Your breath is a slow,
soft breeze.
Your heart is an
open window.

*Acceptance does
not mean approval.
Acceptance is the
willingness to
acknowledge what is,
and then make mindful
choices from there.*

Just do the next thing.

Gazing into a flower is the essence of life moving forward.

Sometimes it takes the intense color of a flower to recognize the mystery of Mother Nature.

Happiness is beneficial for the body, but it is grief that develops the powers of the mind.

We each have our own story, but we also have the power to change that story any time.

Experience deep connection and relaxation in body, mind, and spirit.

Each of your five senses is a gift.
Learn to feel at home in your body.

The older we get, the more we should embrace gratitude.
Every milestone passed is worthy of celebration.

If there are rocks in your path, step over them to find the beauty in life.

True life is lived when tiny changes occur.

Great things are achieved one step at a time.

To be mindful is to live moment by moment,
greeting each moment as if it were ripe for the picking.

The practice of mindfulness requires great patience and a flood of compassion.

What I think and what I feel dictate how I live my life.

Not all of life's mysteries need to be solved,
but all of life's wonders need to be treasured.

Practice gratitude.
I am grateful for the abundance of colors life offers me.

Ambiguity is a part of life.
Things do not always have to be clear to be useful or beautiful.

Stop. Breathe. Look up. Be humbled.

Moon, Moon, beautiful Moon.
Fill it up, fill it up, fill it up.

No matter where you are or what the season,
nature is the greatest show on Earth.

Tears should be welcomed, not avoided.
They were created for release and renewal.

Choose what to focus on, and give it your undivided attention.

Life is more meaningful when your physical, emotional, spiritual, social,
and intellectual components come together in balance.

Resilience isn't just how we bounce back from challenges or tough times.
It is also about how we prepare ourselves for them.

During meditation, observe each thought and then let it go,
like a leaf floating by in a stream.

Celebrate life through the lens of gratitude.

Even the smallest things in nature are extraordinary.

Face your fears of not being in control.
Many challenges can be met only by reaching out and working with others.

Eat with intention.
Be grateful for what is laid before you.

Failure always clears a path toward growth.

Creating balance in your life is not about standing perfectly still.
It is more like swaying, slowing down, and getting stronger.

AFTERWORD

There's a special magic that only a photograph can capture. In many ways, it's the epitome of being in the moment—an image, frozen in time. What we can learn and draw from that stillness is unlike anything that a moving image can communicate. Yet, while collaborating with the world's preeminent nature cinematographer, we clearly couldn't stop there. The accompanying video provides another dimension (or two) to the experience.

Whether you are gliding over mountaintops or peeking into the tiniest of unseen worlds, you'll be taken on a cosmic journey that will leave you breathless. Let the visual feast and powerful music usher you into a meditative state, filled with the kind of awe and gratitude that only nature can inspire.

Inspiration is just the beginning. The impetus behind this endeavor is also about healing. Did you know that 80 percent of the information you receive comes through your eyes? Traditionally, however, it's this visual component that is missing in most wellness experiences. Research has shown that viewing soothing images of nature reduces stress by lowering pulse rate, respiration rate, and blood pressure. Nature allows you to become more "in spirit," renewed, and reconnected.

We envision a not-too-distant future when the power of visual energy could be used in hospitals and nursing homes to comfort and heal patients. And, as we've encouraged here, the use of visual healing with the practice of mindfulness can help to keep us well—a sort of preventive medicine of the soul.

If the images of nature found in this book and video, paired thoughtfully with our Mindful Intentions, have enabled you to find peace, balance, and even healing, we are grateful to have realized our own Mindful Intention. Thank you for allowing us the opportunity.

ACKNOWLEDGMENTS

Miraval wishes to acknowledge everyone who helped make this book go from a simple idea to the reality it is. Each beautiful page invites readers to step into the magic that mindfulness can create. Marrying Louie's breathtaking photography to our contributors' astute words all speaks to Miraval's mission of living in the moment.

We sincerely wish to thank Louie Schwartzberg, Michael Tompkins, Scott James, Mary Monaghan, Leeann Ray, Leigh Weinraub, Molly Stranahan, Wyatt Webb, Randy Flora, Junelle Lupiani, Anne Parker, Sheryl Brooks, Neil McLeod, and Andrew Wolf.

In addition, this entire book would not have been possible without the dedication and fortitude of Sharon Rapoport at Left Brain | Right Brain for her writing skills, creative mind, and open heart.

Louie Schwartzberg wishes to acknowledge the friends who co-created this book, including Michael Tompkins, Sharon Rapoport, Courtney Earlywine, Sara Ramo, and Scott James.

And, a special note of gratitude to Mother Nature, who taught him everything about lighting, composition, and mindfulness.

Louie Schwartzberg is a visual artist breaking barriers, connecting with audiences, and telling stories that celebrate life and reveal the mysteries and wisdom of nature, people, and places.

Louie takes audiences on journeys through distance and time, helping us to truly see our world—its vast swaths of beauty and its smallest miracles—while inspiring humanity to become more responsible caretakers of this fragile planet we all share.

Louie's film shorts and TED Talks have garnered over 37 million views. His recent projects include the movie *Wings of Life* with Disneynature, narrated by Meryl Streep; *Mysteries of the Unseen World*, a 3-D IMAX film with National Geographic; and the *Moving Art* original series for Netflix. Oprah featured a one-hour interview with Louie in the spring of 2014 on her *Super Soul Sunday* program.

His stunning imagery has enhanced films by directors Steven Spielberg, Oliver Stone, Francis Ford Coppola, Paul Haggis, Ridley Scott, and more. Over his long trailblazing career, Louie has earned myriad awards and honors including two Clio Awards, an Emmy nomination for Best Cinematography, and numerous film festival prizes.

He has founded Moving Art™, the first collection of 2-D and 3-D moving images created as fine art for digital screens, from nature to cityscapes to visual effects—all designed to inspire, educate, and perhaps even evolve our perspective on the world. Moving Art™ can be found practically everywhere, from your local theater to the smart phone in your pocket to your home via Roku, Xbox, and Netflix. As part of the solution to nature deficit disorder, Louie is designing immersive sight and sound **visual healing** experiences in select hospitality and spa venues worldwide. Millions of people around the globe have gained an appreciation for the natural world through the images of Louie Schwartzberg. His greatest mission is to make us all protect and celebrate life. Learn more at movingart.com.

There are spas . . . and then there is *Miraval.*

Miraval means "view of the valley," a poignant name for this exclusive desert retreat nestled in the foothills of the Santa Catalina Mountains just north of Tucson, Arizona. And although some trips take you to places you've never been before, even to destinations that few others have ever seen, Miraval Resort & Spa offers the most inspiring getaway one can imagine—a journey unique to everyone who visits.

Consistently rated among the world's top spas and resorts by TripAdvisor and SpaFinder and publications such as *Travel+Leisure, Celebrated Living*, and *Condé Nast Traveler*, Miraval has earned its trendsetting reputation as America's destination for life betterment, where guests feel, are, and can be more.

Since its beginning in 1995, Miraval has upheld a powerfully simple vision: *Life is more meaningful and enjoyable when your physical, emotional, spiritual, social, and intellectual components are in balance.* To that end, Miraval offers more than 100 unique life-enhancing programs and activities. Guests plan their stay filled with an abundance of choices, including innovative spa treatments, self-discovery activities led by insightful well-being specialists, dynamic growth and development programs, outdoor challenges, yoga and Pilates, stress-management techniques, and nutritional counseling. All aim to help people better manage our fast-paced world and life's daily demands.

Guests from around the world relish the resort not only for its luxury, but also for the deep comfort they can find nowhere else—speaking to Miraval's authentic wish for every guest: *You won't find you anywhere else.*
www.MiravalResorts.com

PHOTOGRAPH INFORMATION

Cover, Rincon Beach, California

Title page, Christmas cactus flower

Contents page, hummingbird, Santa Rita Ridge, Panama

p. i, slot canyon, Arizona

p. xii, Rincon Beach, California

p. 2, Big Sur, California

p. 3, Big Sur, California

p. 4, Big Sur, California

p. 5, Big Sur, California

p. 6, Queen Victoria agave

p. 7, orangutan, Java, Indonesia

p. 8, Big Sur, California

p. 9, Bandaloop Dancers, Marin, California

p. 10, nectar bat, Bahia de Kino, Mexico

p. 11, Rincon Beach, California

p. 12, Vancouver, British Columbia

p. 13, Page, Arizona

p. 14, Big Sur, California

p. 15, Niagara Falls, Ontario, Canada

p. 16, Jardin Des Tuileries, ferris wheel, Paris, France

p. 17, Daytona Beach, Florida

p. 18, apple orchard, Tetbury, England

p. 19, Canna "Durban" leaf

p. 20, Seal Harbor, Maine

p. 21, Rincon Beach, California

p. 22, subway train, Brussels, Belgium

p. 23, train station, England

p. 24, Mercer Island, Washington State

p. 25, Rincon Beach, California

p. 26, Rincon Beach, California

p. 27, bumblebee pollinating flower

p. 28, Yosemite National Park, California

p. 29, Big Sur, California

p. 30, pink-and-yellow orchid

p. 31, purple water lily, Hawaii

p. 32, Hawaii waterfall

p. 33, Yosemite National Park, California

p. 34, Rincon Beach, California

p. 35, orange rose

p. 36, Yosemite National Park, California

p. 37, Waipio Valley, Hawaii

p. 38, pumpkin patch, New Hampshire

p. 39, the Alps, Switzerland

p. 40, the Grand Teton, Wyoming

p. 41, Rincon Beach, California

p. 42, Olympic National Park, Washington State

p. 43, Haleakala, Hawaii

p. 44, New Orleans

p. 45, hummingbird, Santa Rita Ridge, Panama

p. 46, monarch butterflies, El Rosario, Mexico

p. 47, Iguazu Falls, Brazil

p. 48, Joshua Tree, California

p. 49, monarch butterflies, El Rosario, Mexico

p. 50, island near Fiji

p. 51, atop Sydney Harbor Bridge, Sydney, Australia

p. 52, dolphin, Rincon, California

p. 53, Golden Gate Bridge, San Francisco, California

p. 54, Los Angeles, California

p. 55, Elk, California

p. 56, Chicago, Illinois

p. 57, monarch butterflies, Lawrence, Kansas

p. 58, Telluride, Colorado

p. 59, Ilulissat, Greenland

p. 60, Ilulissat, Greenland

p. 61, barrel cactus, Tucson, Arizona

p. 62, Grand Canyon, Utah

p. 63, elephants, Africa

p. 64, dewdrops on petal of purple pansy

p. 65, poppies, Big Sur, California

p. 66, Taj Mahal, India

p. 67, Prague astronomical clock, Czech Republic

p. 68, dandelion

p. 69, Waipio, Hawaii

p. 70, pink grasshopper, New Orleans

p. 71, Ilulissat, Greenland

p. 72, Waipio, Hawaii

p. 73, Studio City, California

p. 74, cactus, Tucson, Arizona

p. 75, slot canyon, Arizona

p. 76, Waipio, Hawaii

p. 77, dew on stamen of purple pansy

p. 78, Olympia, Washington State

p. 79, highway in Brussels, Belgium

p. 80, subway train, Brussels, Belgium

p. 81, Maui, Hawaii

p. 82, London, England

p. 83, Maui, Hawaii

p. 84, Yosemite National Park, California

p. 85, Vancouver, British Columbia

p. 86, Anthurium "Flamingo Flower"

p. 87, wildflowers, Sundance, Utah

p. 88, Rincon Beach, California

p. 89, Ilulissat, Greenland

p. 90, birdbath, India

p. 91, river near Iguazu Falls, Brazil

p. 92, Mumbai, India

p. 93, Mumbai, India

p. 94, Mumbai, India

p. 95, Rainbow Bridge National Monument, Utah

p. 96, Rincon Beach, California

p. 97, Big Sur, California

p. 98, pink lotus, Tetbury, England

p. 99, yellow gaillardia flower

p. 100, raccoons, Vancouver, British Columbia

p. 101, Japanese section of Huntington Botanical Garden, Pasadena, California

p. 102, Paris, France

p. 103, aspens, Telluride, Colorado

p. 104, Vancouver, British Columbia

p. 105, Mumbai, India

p. 106, Mumbai, India

p. 107, Vermont

p. 108, amaryllis

p. 109, dewdrops on purple pansy

p. 110, Yosemite National Park, California

p. 111, El Morro, San Juan, Puerto Rico

p. 112, Grenadines, Caribbean

p. 113, Studio City, California

p. 114, moose, Jackson Hole, Wyoming

p. 115, Rincon Beach, California

p. 116, honeybee pollinating yellow gaillardia flower

p. 117, London, England

p. 118, wild berries, Maine

p. 119, Tucson, Arizona

p. 120, Ponte Vecchio Bridge, Florence, Italy

p. 121, Jackson Hole, Wyoming

p. 122, Puna, Peru

p. 123, succulent flower

p. 124, Maui, Hawaii

p. 125, moon, Santa Barbara, California

p. 126, Ilulissat, Greenland

p. 127, dewdrops on nasturtium leaf

p. 128, pink-and-white dahlia

p. 129, Page, Arizona

p. 130, Monument Valley, Utah

p. 131, Yosemite National Park, California

p. 132, dew on petal of purple passionflower

p. 133, orchid bees near yellow orchids, Santa Rita Ridge, Panama

p. 134, bumblebees in nest, Arizona

p. 135, strawberry

p. 136, Grenadines, Caribbean

p. 137, Cortes Island, British Columbia

We hope you enjoyed this Hay House book. If you'd like to receive our online catalog featuring additional information on Hay House books and products, or if you'd like to find out more about the Hay Foundation, please contact:

Hay House, Inc., P.O. Box 5100, Carlsbad, CA 92018-5100
(760) 431-7695 or (800) 654-5126
(760) 431-6948 (fax) or (800) 650-5115 (fax)
www.hayhouse.com® • www.hayfoundation.org

———————————————————————

Published and distributed in Australia by: Hay House Australia Pty. Ltd., 18/36 Ralph St., Alexandria NSW 2015 • Phone: 612-9669-4299 • Fax: 612-9669-4144 • www.hayhouse.com.au

Published and distributed in the United Kingdom by: Hay House UK, Ltd., Astley House, 33 Notting Hill Gate, London W11 3JQ • Phone: 44-20-3675-2450 • Fax: 44-20-3675-2451 • www.hayhouse.co.uk

Published and distributed in the Republic of South Africa by: Hay House SA (Pty), Ltd., P.O. Box 990, Witkoppen 2068 • Phone/Fax: 27-11-467-8904 • www.hayhouse.co.za

Published in India by: Hay House Publishers India, Muskaan Complex, Plot No. 3, B-2, Vasant Kunj, New Delhi 110 070 • Phone: 91-11-4176-1620 • Fax: 91-11-4176-1630 • www.hayhouse.co.in

Distributed in Canada by: Raincoast Books, 2440 Viking Way, Richmond, B.C. V6V 1N2
Phone: 1-800-663-5714 • Fax: 1-800-565-3770 • www.raincoast.com

———————————————————————

Take Your Soul on a Vacation

Visit www.HealYourLife.com® to regroup, recharge, and reconnect with your own magnificence. Featuring blogs, mind-body-spirit news, and life-changing wisdom from Louise Hay and friends. Visit www.HealYourLife.com today!

FREE E-NEWSLETTERS
FROM HAY HOUSE, THE ULTIMATE
RESOURCE FOR INSPIRATION

Be the first to know about Hay House's dollar deals, free downloads, special offers, affirmation cards, giveaways, contests, and more!

 Get exclusive excerpts from our latest releases and videos from *Hay House Present Moments*.

 Enjoy uplifting personal stories, how-to articles, and healing advice, along with videos and empowering quotes, within *Heal Your Life*.

 Have an inspirational story to tell and a passion for writing? Sharpen your writing skills with insider tips from *Your Writing Life*.

Sign Up Now!

Get inspired, educate yourself, get a complimentary gift, and share the wisdom!

http://www.hayhouse.com/newsletters.php

VISIT **www.hayhouse.com** TO SIGN UP TODAY!

 HAY HOUSE   HAYHOUSE RADIO *radio for your soul*   HealYourLife.com